Original title:
The Green Groaners

Copyright © 2025 Creative Arts Management OÜ
All rights reserved.

Author: Lorenzo Barrett
ISBN HARDBACK: 978-1-80567-388-0
ISBN PAPERBACK: 978-1-80567-687-4

The Pained Petals' Serenade

Petals quiver in the breeze,
Wincing like they've stubbed a toe.
They dance in jigs, with slight unease,
Whispering secrets only flowers know.

Bees buzz by with frantic glee,
Mocking blooms in silly flight.
'Why so blue? Come laugh with me,'
Say the pollen-laden pests tonight.

Daffodils in bright despair,
Attempting to mend their wrinkled seams.
"Oh dear, watch the wind! We're quite the pair,"
As gardeners plot their nightly schemes.

But amid this raucous, funny plight,
Petals clink like glasses in a toast,
They toast to friends in silly fright,
Accidental heroes, they enjoy the most.

Melodies of Morose Moss

Moss sings songs of dampened cheer,
Echoing woes from the forest floor.
With every note, they shed a tear,
Moaning tales of soggy lore.

Beneath the trees, they form a band,
With fallen leaves as their fine drum.
A thumping beat, the swamp does stand,
While critters join with a joyful hum.

"Why so sad?" chirps a sprightly frog,
"Join our fun, life's a froggy dream!"
The moss replies with a heavy grog,
In their kingdom of moss, spirits seem to beam.

Yet in their tunes of whimsical grief,
They find delight in rainy days.
Though life may seem beyond belief,
Moss knows humor in muddy ways.

Shadows of the Stalwart Saplings

Saplings stretching, arms held wide,
Strain to catch the sunlight's grace.
In playful jest, they often bide,
Standing tall, yet longing for a race.

"Who will grow up, sprout, and sway?"
Chirps a sparrow from its seat.
"Race to the clouds, don't get gray,
You'll tip over, and then?! Oops, repeat!"

The eldest branch begins to dance,
In stylish moves, it twirls around.
"Come join me, give it a chance,
Let's sashay without a sound!"

Though shadows stretch in all their stance,
They giggle as the wind takes flight.
Saplings dream of their big chance,
To one day glow in dazzling light.

The Grit of Gnarled Roots

Roots entwined in tangled fate,
Beneath the soil, they wiggle and squirm.
"Hey there, buddy, let's just wait,
For worms to dance and their stories confirm."

The wise roots grumble, twist, and bend,
"Oh, to stretch above ground would be great!"
But with a laugh, they know, my friend,
They hold the earth, so won't complain of fate.

"Let's share some laughs with the dirt in tow,"
Said one to another with a gregarious grin.
"Nothing quite like a worm's funny show,
To lighten the soil beneath our skin!"

In the twilight, roots sink in humor,
Knotted tales of moisture and mirth.
With every giggle, they grow in rumor,
Their laughter tickles the heart of the earth.

Secrets of the Somber Shrubs

In the garden where shadows play,
Shrubs whisper secrets in their own way.
They chuckle and giggle in silent glee,
Beneath their leaves, there's silliness to see.

Petals gossip with the breeze each night,
About the deer that gives them a fright.
They wear their green coats with such pride,
Yet all their laughter, they try to hide.

Lament of the Lush Landscape

Oh, how the flowers moan and sigh,
When the bees pass by and say goodbye.
They wish for a chance to take a flight,
But stuck in soil, they can't get it right.

The grass gets jealous, growing so tall,
While daisies roll over in their floral brawl.
With roots so tangled, they can't escape,
A comedy show with each change of shape.

The Sigh of Swollen Stems

Stems stand rigid, puffed with an air,
They act like they just don't have a care.
But bend a little and you might just hear,
A giggle or two mixed with some cheer.

With leaves that rustle, they plot and scheme,
To bust up the garden's snooze-filled dream.
A flower now sneezes, spreading some fun,
While the broccoli chuckles, thinking it's done.

Gloomy Gardens of Grief

In shadowy corners where weeds take root,
A gloomy garden dons its sad pursuit.
With frowning faces, the plants all pout,
Yet their jests can whisper, without a doubt.

Cabbages sulk, with heads hung low,
While carrots giggle, in rows, they grow.
A grumpy old cactus shakes off his blues,
For laughter in gardens, all wear different shoes.

Murmurs in the Meadow

In the meadow, whispers float,
Grassy giggles, a playful note.
Butterflies dance, bees are a buzz,
Nature's laughter, oh what a fuzz!

Daisies chuckle, daisies tease,
Tickled by a warm, gentle breeze.
Caterpillars give a sly wink,
Silly thoughts that make us think.

A cow stumbles, trips on a stone,
Mooing loudly, all on its own.
The flowers nod, in fits they sway,
"Let's have a laugh, it's a good day!"

In this meadow, joy runs wild,
Every leaf, a cheeky child.
With every rustle, jolly and bright,
Nature's giggle fills the night.

Sadness of the Swaying Grass

The grass looks down, it starts to cry,
Tickled toes but oh so shy.
Breezes tease, waves roll high,
"Why's no one dancing? Oh my, oh my!"

Whispering blades mourn in lines,
"Such great heights, but no sunshine shines!"
They envy flowers, standing tall,
With petals bright, they love to brawl.

A rabbit hops, gives a wink,
"Grass, don't fret, come have a drink!"
With dewdrops sweet, they share a cheer,
"Laugh it off, no need for fear!"

Yet still they sway, with a sigh,
Each bend a chuckle, they can't deny.
In their sadness, humor's found,
In every sway, laughter's sound.

Weeping Willows and Heavy Branches

Oh weeping willow, oh why the woe?
Heavy branches move, swinging low.
Leaves like tears, drop with a pout,
Whispering secrets they can't shout.

Tangled twigs tease, a riddle to share,
"Look at me! I may need a chair!"
The laughter echoes, through the night,
Branches dance and twist with delight.

But then a squirrel gets really bold,
Hangs upside down, laughs uncontrolled.
"Dear willow friend, cheer up now please,
For every sadness, just laugh with ease!"

Willow sighs, then starts to sway,
Branches bouncing, feeling the play.
In this grove, joy's mingled with tears,
Tickling trunks, dispelling fears.

The Unheard Chorus of the Thicket

In the thicket, voices hum,
A hidden choir, oh so dumb.
Bushes sway, in soft refrain,
They crack jokes to relieve the pain.

Thorns gossip about the rose,
"Wish I had a dress like those!"
Berries giggle, round and red,
"Join our song, we'll wake the dead!"

Leaves rustle, joining in fun,
"What's the deal? Why the long run?"
A deer prances, gives a glance,
"It's a party! Come join our dance!"

But one old trunk, feeling ignored,
Sighs deeply, 'neath the rewards.
Yet in humor, the thicket thrives,
Laughter grows, and so it strives.

Verdant Whispers

In the patch where vegetables play,
Carrots dabble, turnips sway.
Onions joke about their skin,
Lettuce laughs, oh where to begin!

Tomatoes blushing, growing shy,
Pepper's spicy, aiming high.
They gossip under the sun's gleam,
Dreaming big, living the dream!

Beneath the soil, worms have a ball,
Wiggling away, they have a call.
Radishes tease with their bright hue,
Poking fun at the beet's blue stew!

So next time you stroll down the lane,
Remember their jokes, they're never plain.
A garden's laughter fills the air,
With verdant whispers everywhere!

Lament of the Leafy

In the forest, leaves sigh and groan,
Whispering tales of seeds well-sown.
Why must we dance on a windy spree?
Oh for the days, when none dared flee!

Branches chuckle at squirrels' antics,
Scoffing at their trivial pranks.
Mushrooms grumble, hidden from sight,
While grasses sway with pure delight.

Ferns laugh at old trees' creaks and cracks,
Claiming wisdom, yet hiding snacks.
Saplings pout, longing to grow,
But giggle as the breezes blow!

Yet the leafy ones, vivid and bright,
Whisper their woes in the pale moonlight.
In their lament, a song still rings,
The funny tales that nature sings.

Echoes in the Canopy

Up in the branches where secrets dwell,
Birds share jokes, and all is well.
Critters chuckle at the clouds above,
As the breeze twirls them, oh such love!

Echoes of laughter, a comical sound,
Swinging leaves swirl round and round.
Squirrels debate if acorns are grand,
While owls hoot in their wisdom band.

The sunbeams peek through with a grin,
Dancing with shadows, letting light in.
A chattering chorus plays each day,
Nature's stage where all laugh and play!

The canopy shouts, 'Join the fun!'
With all its stories, second to none.
So next time you wander and roam,
Listen close; the leaves call you home!

Melancholy of Moss

On damp stones, moss gathers round,
Moping softly without a sound.
'Why am I always the underdog?'
Grumbles the clump, stuck in a fog.

With each raindrop, it sighs anew,
'Why can't I grow just like bamboo?'
Yet in shadows, it finds its cheer,
Joining the mushrooms, drawing them near.

The bark beetles laugh at their plight,
"Life's quite funny; get it right!"
Though often hidden, they have their fame,
In tiny worlds, they play the game.

So here's to the moss, a dreary friend,
Whose humor comes in potluck blend.
In the softest of greens, they take their stand,
Waving their woes across the land!

Whiny Wisps of Wildflowers

The daisies pout in the light,
Complaining about the birds' flight.
Tulips grumble, feeling shifty,
While peonies sigh, 'It's too drifty!'

Roses moan over yesterday's dew,
As violets argue about the hue.
Sunflowers droop, a dramatic act,
While lilacs grump, 'We need more tact!'

Dandelions blow with a scoff,
'Why must the wind be so rough?'
Buttercups huff, 'This soil's too tight!'
And clovers just dream of the night.

Forget-me-nots giggle with glee,
As blossoms exchange their petty decree.
In the garden, it's a comical scene,
With wildflowers restless and mean.

The Brooding Borders of Biodiversity

In the hedge, the hedgehogs complain,
'Life's too quiet, it's driving us insane!'
The rabbits argue who's too hairy,
While field mice plot, all feeling wary.

The snakes hiss about the stinky weeds,
While frogs croak out their jealous needs.
The owls hoot, 'We need more drama!'
As crickets chirp, 'What's with this karma?'

Bumblebees buzz, creating a ruckus,
While skunks declare, 'Who's more pungent?' There's fuss!
A chipmunk frets, 'These snacks are stale!'
And everyone groans, 'What's our next tale?'

In this vibrant, noisy mess,
Nature's borders are in distress.
Yet somehow in chaos, they'll find a way,
To laugh through their gripes, come what may.

Mournful Echoes in the Evergreen

The pines sway, wrapped in grey thoughts,
Mourning the storms, counting their knots.
Spruce trees sulk in their shady spots,
While firs grumble 'These squirrels are bold blots!'

Cedar sighs in deep, low tones,
Whispering tales of forgotten phones.
Underneath, the mushrooms frown,
As moss gripes, 'We need a crown!'

The lichen grumbles, feeling bland,
'Why can't someone lend us a hand?'
Willow trees mutter about the rain,
As oaks contemplate their last grain.

In this forest of funereal cheer,
Echoes of laughter still seem near.
For even when mournful, they gather to jest,
Finding humor in shadows, they're truly blessed.

Wistful Whispers in the Wilderness

In the thicket, shadows trace a line,
Where echoes murmur, 'Life's too fine!'
The rabbits nibble with distant dreams,
While deers ponder their quiet schemes.

The winds whistle tunes of missed chance,
As chipmunks debate their next dance.
The owls roll their eyes at the crows,
Wondering why they keep striking poses.

Bears snicker at the buzzing bees,
'You're flying around like you're at ease!'
While foxes craft tales of their romps,
Crickets compare their nighttime stomps.

In the wilderness, whispers abound,
With every creature sharing profound.
Through giggles and sighs, they find their delight,
In a comedy of errors, beneath moonlight.

The Sighs of Silken Sprouts

In the garden, things do pout,
Little sprouts are full of clout.
Whispering tales of rainbows weep,
Muttering secrets they can't keep.

One claims to grow a bean so tall,
It will touch the clouds, oh what a fall!
They giggle at the bugs that sneak,
A leafy waltz, so sly and sleek.

With every breeze, a little sigh,
"Will the sun come out?" they cry.
Bantering with the bees nearby,
As the clouds roll in, they shy.

In this patch of green delight,
Even weeds get things just right.
With every tussle with the grass,
So much fun, they let it pass.

Melancholy in the Meadow

In the meadow, flowers weep,
Petals droop and secrets keep.
Each blade of grass has heard it all,
Their tales echo, "Oh, the fall!"

Bees dally on a dandelion,
"Do we dare?" they keep on trying.
The daisies roll their eyes in jest,
"Who's the fairest? It's an endless quest!"

A thistle grumbles, "Life's unfair,
Stuck here with so much bare!"
While a buttercup can't help but grin,
"Smile, my friends, let life begin!"

In the glow of sunlight bright,
They dance in shadows, full of light.
With a flutter and a leap, oh dear,
A meadow full of chuckles near!

The Lament of Leafy Legends

Oh, leafy giants, stand so tall,
Sharing tales of the fall.
Whispers swirl in every breeze,
Of antics past in happy trees.

A brave oak boasting of its age,
Claims to be the wisest sage.
With younger sprouts who laugh and play,
Telling tales of yesterday.

The maples blush, their colors bold,
"Autumn always makes us old!"
While pines just shake their needles free,
"Stay evergreen, who needs a spree?"

In this forest full of cheer,
Legends grow year after year.
Giggles echo with every sway,
At the antics of foliage on display.

A Chorus of Chlorophyll

In the jungles, laughter roars,
Leaves discussing ancient scores.
With vines as ropes and roots to play,
Chlorophyll sings of the day.

Creeping ivy, bold and spry,
Mimics birds that soar and fly.
"Let's have a jam session, come!"
"Only if you bring the drum!"

Ferns fill in with flutes so fine,
As petals dance, how divine!
With flowers clapping in sync,
"What's next, a drink of dew to drink?"

And when the sun begins to set,
The leafy crew won't forget.
With giggles bright till twilight calls,
Nature's music in leafy halls.

Rumbles in the Rhododendron

In the garden where plants plot,
A cabbage sneezes, a flower forgot.
The carrots giggle, the lettuce shakes,
As radishes whisper of secret fakes.

A rose complains of its thorny plight,
Saying, "Why do hugs feel like a fight?"
The daisies dance to a tune unheard,
While broccoli thinks it's a wise old bird.

The daisies whisper, "What's that stench?"
"Oh dear," groans the garlic, "I'm in a wrench!"
A bumblebee laughs, tickled by fate,
While herbs hold court and enjoy the debate.

Underneath it all, a funny scene,
As veggies joke and share the green.
In this leafy world, no sorrow to find,
Just giggles and grumbles, all entwined.

The Unseen Tales of Trees

In the forest where shadows play,
Oaks talk gossip by the light of day.
A whisper drifts from a birch so tall,
"Did you hear what happened to the maple ball?"

Pines pine for sun with a prickly grin,
While willows sway with a swish and spin.
A cedar chuckles, says, "Life is grand!"
Though a young sapling can't quite understand.

Each branch has secrets, oh what a sight,
Twiggy tales told till the fall of night.
Leaves rustle laughter, a whimsical hum,
And roots below mimic the bass drum.

With the wind as muse, stories unfold,
Of acorns and squirrels, both brave and bold.
In the fabric of green, joy intertwines,
Among the old trees, every day shines.

Nature's Discontent

The daisies frowned, huddled in fear,
Of snails who took too long, oh dear!
The daisies moaned for some speedier eats,
While the earthworms chuckled, doing their feats.

A thunderstorm rumbled, a squirrel stood still,
As the puddles gathered, nature's own thrill.
The tulips cried, "Why don't we dance?"
But their roots were stuck, missed the chance.

The sun peeped out, gave a cheeky grin,
As the clouds debated who'd go back in.
In this wild drama, life's full of jest,
With each little grumble, they try their best.

So nature sighs in a whimsical way,
Finding joy in each rainy day.
With laughter echoing, oh, what a blend,
Nature's discontent is just a trend!

Sorrow in the Sycamore

A sycamore sighed, leaned low with a frown,
For critters were teasing, all over town.
"Why must they mock my balding crown?"
The squirrels just giggled, flipping around.

The sparrows chirped of a nest too snug,
While a crow swooped down, giving a shrug.
"Who knew stress could come from such little things?"
As the sycamore wondered about plump winged kings.

In the breeze it swayed, still trying to think,
Of the daisies' sass and the roses' wink.
The bark whispered tales of a softer dawn,
As laughter erupted in the dew-dappled lawn.

Yet despite its woes and leafy distress,
The sycamore chuckled at its own mess.
For in this wild patch of a funny folklore,
There's never a dull day, not even once more.

Harsh Harmonies in the Hedges

In the hedge, a crow does croak,
With a tune that makes dogs choke.
The bushes shiver, leaves in fright,
As the feline choir sings at night.

A hedgehog hums with great delight,
Trying to join in the feathered fight.
Squirrels giggle at the sound,
While bushes bounce and sway around.

Gnomes in gardens lose their cool,
As flowers dance, it's quite the fool.
Daffodils sigh, while tulips blush,
In the noise of this glorious hush.

Everyone joins in, what a mess,
Nature's orchestra, a big excess.
But in the end, they all agree,
It's best just to let chaos be.

Plight of the Pining Pines

Pines lament in a windy jest,
Whispering secrets, not at rest.
Branches sway, an awkward dance,
With squirrels giggling, taking a chance.

One pine shouts, "I'm taller, you fool!"
"Yeah, but your needles are a drool!"
They tumble and tease with giddy glee,
While weary birds complain, "Oh me!"

A beetle rolls by, a punster true,
Says, "Pine trees, you've got a view!"
The sap drips down with a sticky laugh,
Nature's comedy, the lumbering staff.

Through all the strife and cheeky banter,
The pines stay strong, an evergreen canter.
With every gust, they proudly shine,
Cheering each other, one big pine line.

Woe in the Willow's Wail

Willow weeps in the twilight glow,
With branches dragging, oh so slow.
"Why so blue?" the fox did tease,
"Life's too short to just appease!"

"Oh hush!" cried Willow, "Get off my case!
I've seen more drama than most in this place."
The bumblebees buzzed a merry rhyme,
While daisies shared tales of their prime.

In the shadows, the owls conspire,
Plotting to raise the tension higher.
But laughter erupts from a nearby pond,
With frogs croaking tunes that go far beyond.

Willow finally chuckles and lets out a sigh,
"Laughter's the best, oh me, oh my!"
Her branches sway with rhythm and cheer,
In the heart of the night, a new life appears.

Restless Rumbles of the Rain

Raindrops drum on the window pane,
As clouds convene for a rowdy game.
Puddles form with a splashing sound,
While snails parade, all plump and round.

The thunder growls a grumpy tune,
While lightning flickers like a loony boon.
Dancing drops tap-dance on cars,
Making each vehicle sing with stars.

The flowers shake off a gentle cry,
"Oh why, oh why, must you make us sigh?"
Yet every splash brings life anew,
With giggles shared from birds' avenue.

So let it rain, let it pour,
We'll laugh together, forevermore.
For every storm that stirs and sways,
Bright rainbows blossom on sunny days.

The Gloomy Greenhouse

Inside the glass, a secret hint,
Where cacti dance and onions squint.
A celery sighs, a cucumber frowns,
While carrots debate their leafy crowns.

The humidity thickens like a heavy stew,
As lettuce chuckles in brilliant hue.
Peppers gossip, green with envy,
While poor ole' parsley feels a bit bendy.

Nasturtiums put on a dramatic show,
While weeds play limbo, oh what a flow.
Tomatoes grin in a plastic chair,
Sipping dew drops, without a care.

But wait, what's that? A snail on the prowl,
He slips on lettuce, oh what a howl!
The greenhouse roars with plant-like cheer,
As veggies tumble, not showing fear.

Twinges in the Thyme

Thyme in the garden, a curious bunch,
They giggle at sage through their herbal crunch.
Rosemary rolls her eyes in jest,
While oregano claims, 'I'm the very best.'

Parsley attempts a cool, sly spin,
But basil keeps whispering, 'Where have you been?'
The time ticks slow, the pests start to dance,
As veggies unite for a wild romance.

Mint makes a scene, with fragrance so bold,
While garlic, the joker, starts acting old.
Fennel is giggling, a cheeky root,
Twirling in soil, in a veggie suit.

But soon a voice from the far garden calls,
'Join us for laughter as evening falls.'
A twinge in the thyme, a snippet of cheer,
In the silly garden, no shame, no fear.

Whirl of Wistful Weeds

In the corner of the yard, the weeds take flight,
With dandelions raving through the night.
Clover's got tunes that make the breeze swing,
While thistles pop popcorn and burst into spring.

They dance in circles, a rambunctious crew,
With root beer floats made of morning dew.
Burdock capers, wild and free,
While crabgrass croons a silly spree.

A thistle with flair takes the center stage,
As grasshoppers leap, free from their cage.
Blades twist and twirl, like carefree dreams,
In a whirl of giggles, laughter beams.

Yet, at dawn, the mower does roam,
The weeds scatter, seeking their home.
But they'll be back, with a cheeky grin,
For what's a yard without a little sin?

The Gnawing Thorns of Time

Among the roses, a twist and a snarl,
The thorns have tales to share and unfurl.
One said, 'Time's a raspberry pie,'
While another just sighed, 'Oh me, oh my!'

Blackberries bicker, twisted and bright,
Comparing their bruises from last night's fight.
The elderflower nods, wise and astute,
While geraniums laugh in their flowery suit.

'Oh thorns, do stay! Please don't grow bare,'
Shouts a shy rose, with a delicate flair.
Yet prickled by time, they get quite perturbed,
In a garden of giggles, their laughter curbed.

But when the sun sets and night gives a wink,
The thorns dance freely, without time to think.
Their gnawing need fades, as stars start to chime,
In the whimsical world of the thorns of time.

Shadows of Shimmering Foliage

In a garden where gnomes dance,
Leaves chuckle, taking a chance.
Bumblebees with wigs so bright,
Tickle flowers till they take flight.

Butterflies play hide and seek,
Waiting for the silly peak.
Rabbits hop in jester's garb,
Making every moment a barb.

Clouds drift in a playful race,
While vines curl up, just to chase.
Mossy rocks wear goofy grins,
Laughing at the squirrels' spins.

Nature's stage, a comical sight,
Where every shadow shares a light.
Beneath the trees, the giggles bloom,
In a world where laughter finds room.

The Regretful Blooms

Petals sigh in colors bold,
Wishing for tales left untold.
Daisies pout with frilly crowns,
Whining softly, wearing frowns.

Tulips try to strike a pose,
But end up tangled with their those.
In the wind, they twist and sway,
Murmuring about yesterday.

Rosy blush of life's embrace,
Yet thorns poke with a smiling face.
Every bloom with stories dire,
Regrets wrapped in leafy attire.

Bees buzz past, they strut and brag,
While blossoms spill their woes in rag.
Fragrant airs cloak silly fears,
As petals weep in joyful tears.

Pain of the Petals

Petals whine with each sharp breeze,
Yelling out for fewer tease.
A sunbeam lands on wilting leaves,
While fragrant blooms play practical thieves.

Dandelions grit their teeth,
Fearing clowns who seek some beef.
Hilarious hopes to dodge the rain,
They joke about their aching pain.

Hyacinths request a break,
From garden stakes that make them ache.
Caught beneath a heavy spade,
They laugh it off, though dreams may fade.

A bumblebee lets out a giggle,
As flowers shake, they twist and wiggle.
In a ruckus of petal glee,
The pain seems bland; they laugh with glee.

Grief in the Glade

In the shade where shadows plot,
A squirrel with worries, not a lot.
He frets and frowns under the trees,
While leaves engage in whispered tease.

A toad croaks tales of days long gone,
With a voice that moans like a yawn.
Mossy stones chime in despair,
Yet find hilarity in thin air.

Twisted branches hold their heads low,
Yet each sigh brings a droll flow.
Flowers snicker at the gloom,
Filling the air with leaf-shaped zoom.

Underneath the sorrowful sigh,
A comical tinkle drifts by.
For in every tearful leave,
There's a chuckle urging to believe.

Wistful Wanderings of the Woods

In the heart of the woods, a squirrel's delight,
Chasing his tail like a bumbling kite.
Acorns are falling, like piñata spills,
While branches above play tricks and frills.

Mossy rocks giggle underfoot,
As I trip over roots and feel a hoot.
The breeze whispers secrets, a nonsensical song,
Nature's own band, playing all day long.

Birds in their nests, they chuckle and chirp,
While down below, I tumble and blurb.
Laughter erupts from the bushes and trees,
As I dance with the shadows, all wobbly with glee!

So I wander the woods, lost in the jest,
With critters and laughter, I count them the best.
In every green nook, a giggle I hear,
The woods are alive, and I'm glad to be here!

Twinge of the Tangle

In a thicket where twigs intertwine tight,
A hedgehog rolls over—oh, what a fright!
Branches wrap round like a playful vine,
While I navigate knots that look quite divine.

A rabbit pops out, with a grin on his face,
Singing a jingle, he's in such a race.
Leaves start to rustle, they join in the fun,
As I find myself tangled—oh, here comes the sun!

Rabbits and hedgehogs hold a wild show,
With laughter and antics that never say no.
They twist and they turn, in this merry old game,
In this lively old tangle, they're all so insane!

But alas, I just can't help but to trip,
In a cloak of green, I dare take a dip.
Each step leads to snickers, each leap leads to cheer,
In this tangle of giggles, I feel giddy here!

A Cry in the Greenery

A call from the bushes, an odd little wail,
A creature is fussing, I hope it's not frail!
What lurks in the shadows, with branches for hair?
An owl in a tutu, oh my, what a scare!

The trees stand in silence, but chuckles abound,
As ferns form a chorus, with whimsy profound.
"Come dance with us, hoot!" they chant with delight,
While I try to stifle a involuntary fright.

A raccoon in a top hat joins in the fray,
With hilarious antics, he steals the display.
Laughter erupts from the critters so near,
A cry in the greenery brings joy and good cheer!

So I join in their frolic, embracing the fun,
As nature's own theater performs just for one.
Each rustling leaf sings a merry refrain,
In this green little world, I'll never complain!

Burdened Buds and Blighted Branches

Burdened buds dangle, looking oh so forlorn,
While blighted branches creak like they're worn.
A droopy old flower throws shade at the breeze,
As petals drop down, with the greatest of ease.

"Oh, what a disaster!" the daisies all shout,
As the winds weave a tale of a silly old drought.
With laughter they sway, in a comical line,
While their neighbor, the weed, thinks it looks just fine.

A bush starts to giggle, in a moss-covered trance,
With twigs that shake freely, joining the dance.
So burdened and blighted, they find a bright jest,
In the midst of their woes, they've found laughter's nest.

As I stroll through this landscape, absurd to behold,
I chuckle at petals, their stories unfold.
For nature, though gloomy, has a giggle to spare,
In burlesque of blooms, joy dances in air!

Agonies Among the Apple Boughs

The apples hang with a heavy sigh,
They whisper about the pies nearby.
A squirrel schemes, munching seeds galore,
While branches groan, 'We can't take more!'

The breeze runs through like a tricky thief,
Tickling leaves, causing fruity grief.
Beneath the tree, jokes get tossed,
As ripened fruit counts all the cost.

Each laugh echoes through the orchard wide,
While worms in the core begin to hide.
'Not a single bite!' the boughs lament,
As cider dreams swirl and ferment.

So here's to the fruits, so round and red,
With worries of pies dancing in their head.
Forget the bother, it's all in fun,
Let's make these groans sing, one by one!

The Devil's Details in the Dew

Morning light paints the grass with spite,
As droplets form, they laugh at night.
Each glint is a trick, a mischievous tease,
While shadows waltz among the trees.

Frogs break into a croaking song,
'Why sit in silence when you can't go wrong?'
And snails slide forth on their slippery paths,
Plotting their ways with giggles and laughs.

The devil's in the details, they say,
As dew drops sparkle, giggling away.
A bumblebee buzzes, "I'll steal that sip!"
While ladybugs plan their next little trip.

So watch the morning, full of gleeful cheer,
For the devil delights in the humor here.
With each drop of dew, a world does unfold,
In mists and mirth, stories are told!

Dismal Dreams of Dappled Light

Beneath the branches, shadows sway,
Dreams of sunbeams play their way.
A hint of grumpiness stirs the air,
As squirrels complain of life's unfair.

'Why can't we wear a crown of rays?'
Murmurs one as he counts the ways.
Dappled light dances, igniting the gloom,
While gloomier thoughts find their room.

With every flicker, mischief ensues,
As critters chuckle at their own reviews.
'Unfair!' they scoff, though they jest,
Finding humor in nature's test.

So laugh at the shadows, embrace the night,
For every dim moment holds a bit of light.
In dismal dreams, find the bright and bold,
Twists in the tale we have yet to unfold.

Resentful Roots of Regrowth

Down below where the soil grumbles,
Roots clash and clash, while the ground just humbles.
'Why should we share this patch of worth?'
They grumble and grump as they plot their berth.

New sprouts giggle, 'We'll take the sun!'
As old roots argue, 'This isn't fun!'
They trade their complaints for the soil's embrace,
And ponder the beauty of this green space.

A worm rolls by, with a cheeky grin,
'Just light up, friends, it's a win-win!'
Beneath the surface, a comedy unfolds,
With every twinge, a story told.

So here's to the roots that might seem distressed,
Chasing sunshine, seeking only the best.
With laughs from below, they all take a stand,
In this wiggly world, together they land!

Nature's Nuanced Nonsense

In the garden, gnomes do dance,
Wobbling round like pals in pants.
Flowers giggle, grass takes a bow,
Bees buzz jokes, oh what a crow!

Lettuce whispers, 'Don't tell a soul,
I once played poker with a mole.'
Tomato blushed, said, 'I can't lose,
Last week I dated a pair of shoes!'

Vines sing softly of their long dreams,
Of sunshine naps and silver streams.
The sun gave a wink, the moon a smirk,
Nature's pranksters at work with a quirk.

Oh, the chaos of critters so spry,
Chasing clouds that drift on by.
With a riddle and tickle, they scheme,
To turn our world into a meme!

Verdant Voices Unveiled

In the meadow, a frog has a fit,
Jumping high with a comedic split.
The daisies read fortunes, all unsure,
While the wind spreads rumors—they're never pure.

A worm in a top hat, quite the sight,
Addresses the ants with sheer delight.
'You're all invited to tea,' he beams,
But they just roll eyes, 'Not in our dreams!'

Cacti gossip, they poke with pride,
Sharing secrets of how they can hide.
Under a cactus, they pull a prank,
'Why did the flower join the tank?'

In this playful realm, no gloom in sight,
Nature's folly brings pure delight.
From chuckles of trees to laughter of bees,
Life's a circus, with antics like these!

Growling in the Garden

A squirrel struts with swagger so bold,
Stealing seeds like a pirate of old.
The carrots complain, 'This isn't fair!'
While pumpkins plot to give him a scare.

In shadows, the mushrooms whisper away,
'Who knew gardening could lead to dismay?'
Petunias roll over, waving their heads,
'Let's scare him off—we'll scare him to shreds!'

Vines twine tightly, forming a band,
Giggling 'bout dirt beneath their stand.
Frogs croak rock songs under the moon,
While crickets join in, a vibrant tune.

Rabbits snicker, plotting their next spree,
Chewing on lettuce, 'It's just so free!'
With growls and giggles, all flora and fauna,
Dance to the chaos, their biggest drama!

Echoes of Emerald Envy

A leaf quakes, 'Look at me shine!
I'm brighter than that old pine!'
But the pine just chuckles, rooted in place,
In this leafy rivalry, there's no disgrace.

Crickets chirp, 'We play the best tunes,
Under stars, beneath the moons.'
While daisies nod, 'But we smell just fine,'
Eager to win this fragrant design.

Thorns boast, 'We keep out the fools!'
But in their shadow, forget all the rules.
Petals flutter, 'Why fight for the crown?
Let's bloom together, let's never frown!'

Amidst the laughter and shades of green,
Nature's jesters paint quite the scene.
In this playful squabble, joy takes its flight,
Emerald echoes of pure delight!

Sighs from the Soil

In the garden down below,
Where veggies mumble low,
Carrots wear a frown today,
As dirt gets in the way.

Radishes roll their eyes in red,
Whispers of the lettuce spread,
'Why do we always have to grow,
When all we want is a little glow?'

The beans do awkward dance routines,
Wiggling in their green costumes,
While peas just sit, and softly pout,
Count the clouds that drift about.

But with the sun, hope starts to bloom,
And laughter chases off the gloom,
A party sprouts from seed to sprout,
And nature finds a way to shout!

Verdure's Forgotten Song

The grass sings low of days gone by,
With every rustle, a curious sigh,
'We used to dance beneath the moon,
Now it's just weeds that make us swoon!'

The daisies giggle, a little too loud,
Calling to the dandelions proudly bowed,
'We were the stars, once graceful and bright,
Now we're just fluff in the morning light!'

Thistles lounge, with thorns on display,
Whispering jokes in their prickly way,
'Why take life so serious, dear?
A poke is just laughter we hold near!'

So the leaves join in on the fun,
Bouncing along, hugging the sun,
In harmony, a joyful throng,
Forget the troubles, sing along!

Grief of the Gnarled Roots

Twisted roots beneath the ground,
Mutter tales that swirl around,
'We're stuck in places we can't roam,
No wonder we don't feel at home!'

Old oaks place bets on the squirrels,
While the vines sway, doing twirls,
'We've weathered storms, and that's no lie,
But we can't help it, we still sigh!'

Beneath the bark, the trees discuss,
How to escape this rhyming fuss,
'Can we order some rain for a change?
Or spin dreams that aren't too strange?'

But amidst the grumbles and creaky sound,
Laughter bubbles up from the ground,
For deep in roots, there's life anew,
As joys sprout up to chase the blue!

Tears of the Treetops

From above, the branches weep,
With leaves that dance and secrets keep,
'Why must the clouds be so gray?
Can't we just bask in some sun play?'

Saplings nestle in the breeze,
Whispering tales with childish tease,
'Oh, how we yearn to stretch and soar,
But we're stuck here, longing for more!'

The squirrels play charades on high,
Chasing dreams across the sky,
'Let's dodge raindrops and climb real good,
Pretend we're pirates in the wood!'

Yet in their laughter, hope awakes,
As drops of joy drip, then it breaks,
Turning their tears into silver light,
As they sway and twirl through the night!

The Grief of Greener Pastures

In fields where grass has grown too high,
The cows sit pondering, oh my,
They waited long for tasty snacks,
Now they just plot escape hacks.

The corn stalks laugh, they seem so spry,
While farmers sigh and wonder why,
Tomatoes whisper, full of dread,
As lettuce dreams of being fed.

Faded Dreams in the Ferns

Among the ferns, the dreams decay,
Once bright and green, now dull and gray,
The daisies chat of days gone by,
As weeds just shrug and sigh, oh why?

The ladybugs recall their youth,
When every bug was full of truth,
Now they gossip and complain,
Of faded dreams beneath the rain.

The Echoing Emotions of Evergreens

Evergreens stand tall and proud,
With secrets shared, they speak aloud,
The owls hoot in a witty tone,
While squirrels scheme in barked-out groans.

The pine cones drop, a clumsy dance,
Inviting each to take a chance,
But bears just grunt, so full of fluff,
And grumble that they've had enough.

Tragedy Beneath the Twigs

Underneath the twigs they hide,
The creatures wish they'd take a ride,
On breezes bright, they dream for flight,
But only wish for seeds at night.

The shadows stretch, the sun declines,
While crickets play their silly lines,
In drooping grass, the woes unfold,
As all the jokes grow slightly old.

Echoes of Enigmatic Eden

In a garden filled with chatter,
The veggies grumble loud and clear,
"Why do we end up on a platter?"
"Let's plot our escape from here!"

A carrot whispers to a pea,
"Let's grow legs and run away!"
But lettuce rolls her eyes and sighs,
"We're destined for a salad tray."

Tomatoes blush with fear and glee,
As the chef sharpens his knife,
"Not today, not us," they all agree,
"We'll joke about our leafy strife!"

In this comedic, leafy land,
The humor sprouts, the puns take flight,
Veggies giggle, hand in hand,
In Eden's garden, pure delight.

The Heartache of High Canopies

In the branches, a squirrel sighs,
"My acorns went, oh what a plight!"
He ponders all those frozen fries,
And wishes they would take to flight.

The parrot squawks, a rhyme once penned,
"A fruit bat stole my juicy snack!"
While twigs around lend ears to lend,
Forests echo tales of lack.

As clouds roll by, the leaves all sway,
"Let's throw a party, just for fun!"
But every branch has lost its way,
And none can seem to see the sun.

With laughter tangled, tales unfold,
The canopy will hold its cheer,
For tree-top laughs are purest gold,
In heights where giggles banish fear.

Solitude beneath the Spruce

Beneath the spruce, a snail does twirl,
"I'm faster than I used to be!"
He dreams of racing through the whirl,
Of leaves and acorns, wild and free.

A riddle here, a joke up high,
The pinecones drop with laughter light,
"Why did they sway? Oh my, oh my!
Because the branches tickled right!"

Mossy underpinnings tell of glee,
While roots converge in playful tease,
An acorn shimmies, full of spree,
As laughter breezes through the trees.

Sweet solitude, yet all around,
The life beneath knows how to jest,
In every ring and every sound,
The forest thrives with humor blessed.

Wounded Wisteria

A wisteria weeps with style,
"For blooms and buds, I take my pain."
But vines can only twist and smile,
As butterflies dance in the rain.

"I'm tangled up in love gone wrong,
Munched by munchers, not my type!"
Yet all around the creatures throng,
For chaos sounds a lively pipe.

With petals drooping low with woe,
A bumblebee buzzes in close,
"Let your colors bright, oh glow,
You'll charm them all with art verbose!"

So wounded blooms shake off the drear,
And dazzle like the stars above,
While every laugh and hearty cheer,
Reminds the heart that it's still love.

Cries of the Crumpled Canopies

Leaves rustled high, with a giggle and sigh,
Branches bicker, asking who's next to fly.
The sap drips down, it's a sticky affair,
Nature's own laughter hangs sweet in the air.

Squirrels debating, who gets the first nut,
A raccoon jumps in, "Hey, that's my cut!"
The air fills with chuckles, as creatures collide,
In this leafy circus, no one can hide.

Bright blooms are smirking, their petals alight,
Tickling the breeze, oh what a delight!
While grasses whisper their inaudible jokes,
The garden erupts in two-for-one pokes.

In shadows they wander, with pranks up their sleeves,
Mice playing tag beneath rustling leaves.
Nature's own humor, in every small sound,
In this jolly realm, joy knows no bound.

Gloom Among the Greenery

A cloud of gloom drifts, but don't shed a tear,
The ferns flip a coin to decide who's queer.
A flower exclaims, "My color's the best!"
While violets and daisies all fail the test.

Roots bicker softly, discussing their fate,
"Why do we dig when we could just create?"
A worm pokes his head, sporting a grin,
"Cheer up, lads! Let the fun begin!"

Dandelions laugh as they scatter their seed,
"Who needs a garden? This wind's more our speed!"
A squirrel throws acorns, playing fetch with the breeze,
Oh, but the laughter brings birds to their knees.

So don't mind the gloom that's floating on by,
It's merely a cover for that mischievous sigh.
Underneath all the green, there's a riotous crew,
With joy hidden well, just waiting for you.

Sounds of Swaying Shadows

In twilight's hour, when shadows do sway,
The trees gossip softly, in their leafy café.
Crickets crack jokes, tickling the air,
While fireflies giggle, sparkling everywhere.

A wind with a wiggle, sings songs soft and low,
"What's the fuss about? Just enjoy the show!"
The hidden critters join in with a dance,
Wiggling and wobbling, daring a chance.

Mice in the moonlight, moonwalking with flair,
While moths flap around, like they haven't a care.
Old branches creak on, adding to the tune,
An orchestra playing beneath the fat moon.

So when the night falls, and shadows take flight,
Remember the giggles that echo in the light.
In every rustle, there's a chuckle and cheer,
Nature's sweet laughter brings joy to your ear.

Moans of the Mossy Mirth

Moss cushioned giggles beneath every tread,
As mushrooms chuckle, with faces of red.
A tree trunk complains, "I'm so weary today,"
While vines twist and tangle, "Come join in the play!"

Slugs in a conga, they slide on the ground,
"Why walk when we can just glide all around?"
Leaves whisper gossip, so juicy and fine,
While toads croak along, keeping rhythm in line.

A weathered old rock with stories to spin,
"Kids these days, they just don't know the win!"
But laughter erupts from the undergrowth tight,
The woodland's a playground, alive in the night.

So here in the thicket, where spirits are bright,
Each wobble and wiggle is pure delight.
Embrace all the moans, in mirthful surprise,
For joy's hidden deep, under mossy disguise.

www.ingramcontent.com/pod-product-compliance
Lightning Source LLC
Chambersburg PA
CBHW071813160426
43209CB00003B/66